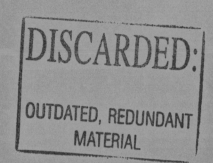

Languages of the World

Spanish

Sarah Medina

Heinemann Library
Chicago, Illinois

www.heinemannraintree.com
Visit our website to find out more information about Heinemann-Raintree books.

To order:

☎ Phone 888-454-2279

🖥 Visit www.heinemannraintree.com to browse our catalog and order online.

©2012 Heinemann Library
an imprint of Capstone Global Library, LLC
Chicago, Illinois

Edited by Dan Nunn, Rebecca Rissman, and
   Catherine Veitch
Designed by Marcus Bell
Picture research by Ruth Blair
Production by Victoria Fitzgerald
Originated by Capstone Global Library Ltd
Printed and bound in China by South China Printing
   Company Ltd

15 14 13 12 11
10 9 8 7 6 5 4 3 2 1

Library of Congress Cataloging-in-Publication Data
Medina, Sarah, 1960-
   Spanish / Sarah Medina.
      p. cm.—(Languages of the world)
   Includes bibliographical references and index.
   ISBN 978-1-4329-5080-4 (hc)—ISBN 978-1-4329-5087-3 (pb) 1. Spanish language—Textbooks for foreign speakers—English. 2. Spanish language—Grammar. 3. Spanish language—Spoken Spanish. I. Title.
   PC4129.E5M453 2012
   468.2'421—dc22   2010043784

Acknowledgments
We would like to thank the following for permission to reproduce photographs: Alamy p. 8 (© carlos sanchez pereyra); Corbis pp. 13 (© Tim Pannell), 21 (© Sam Diephuis), 23 (© Anders Ryman), 29 (© Frederic Soltan); Getty Images pp. 12 (Mel Yates), 24 (Bob Thomas); iStockphoto p. 26 (© Floortje), 27 (© Rob Belknap); Photolibrary pp. 6 (age footstock), 15 (Stock4B), 17 (Somos Images), 18, 19 (Tips Italia), 20 (Blend Images), 25; Shutterstock pp. 5 (© Golden Pixels LLC), 7 (© Stephane Bidouze), 9 (© Andresr), 10 (© blueking), 11 (© silver-john), 14 (© Andy Dean Photography), 16 (© Zoreslava), 22 (© Rob Marmion), 28 (© Mandy Godbehear).

Cover photograph of a pre-teen girl reproduced with permission of Corbis (© Philip Nealey/Somos Images).

We would like to thank Silvia Vázquez Fernández for her invaluable help in the preparation of this book.

Every effort has been made to contact copyright holders of material reproduced in this book. Any omissions will be rectified in subsequent printings if notice is given to the publisher.

Contents

Spanish words are in italics, *like this*. You can find out how to say them by looking in the pronunciation guide.

Spanish Around the World

People first spoke Spanish in Spain, but today Spanish is the main language in 20 countries all around the world. It is also spoken by more than 45 million people in the United States.

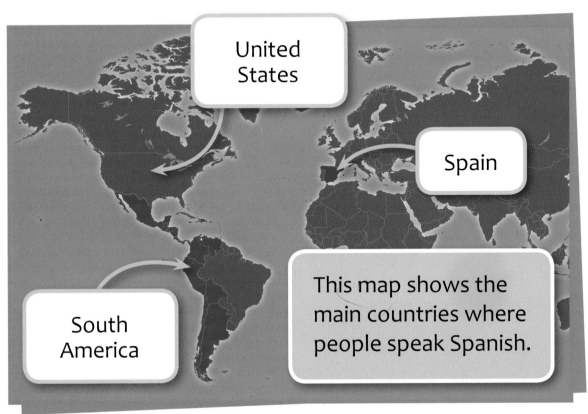

United States

Spain

South America

This map shows the main countries where people speak Spanish.

Even though English is the main language of the United States, millions of Americans speak Spanish at home.

In some Spanish-speaking countries people call Spanish *español*. In others people prefer to call Spanish *castellano*. But *español* and *castellano* are the same language.

Who Speaks Spanish?

Spanish is the main language of about 350 million people around the world. Spanish is the third most spoken language in the world after Mandarin Chinese and English.

Spanish is spoken in most countries in South America.

In Spain, a *carro* is a shopping cart, not a car!

Spanish can sound very different in different countries. People sometimes use different words for the same thing, too. The word for "car" is *coche* in Spain and *carro* in Mexico.

Spanish and English

Some words, like *chocolate*, are spelt the same in Spanish and English. Other words are very similar. Can you guess the meaning of the words below?

bicicleta   fruta   tomate   familia
(See page 32 for answers.)

Ambulancia in Spanish means "ambulance" in English.

Bien cool! means "Really cool!" in Spanglish. *Bien* is Spanish and "cool" is English.

In the United States lots of young people speak "Spanglish." This is a mixture of English and Spanish words. It is like a new language!

Learning Spanish

Spanish uses the same alphabet as English, but it has 29 letters instead of 26. The extra letters are shown in bold below:

a b c **ch** d e f g h i j k l **ll** m n **ñ** o p q r s t u v w x y z

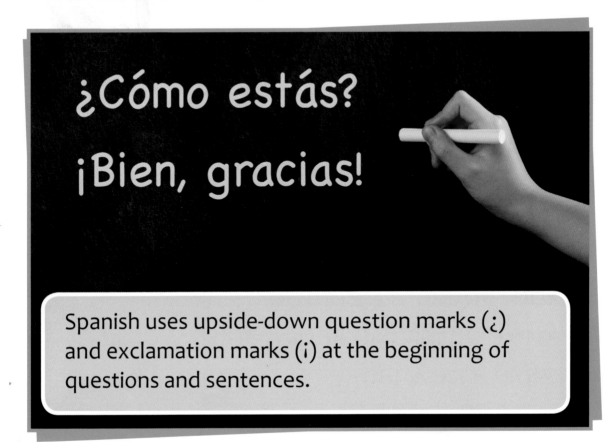

¿Cómo estás?

¡Bien, gracias!

Spanish uses upside-down question marks (¿) and exclamation marks (¡) at the beginning of questions and sentences.

The word "key" in Spanish is *llave*, but you say "ya-bay" with a "y" and a "b", not "la-vay!"

Some letters in the Spanish alphabet sound different to English. In Spain "z" is spoken like "th" in English. In South America, though, "z" sounds like "s."

Saying Hello and Goodbye

Family and friends usually give each other a kiss on the cheek when they say hello. Men might give each other a hug or a pat on the shoulder or back.

How to say it
kiss = *beso*
hug = *abrazo*

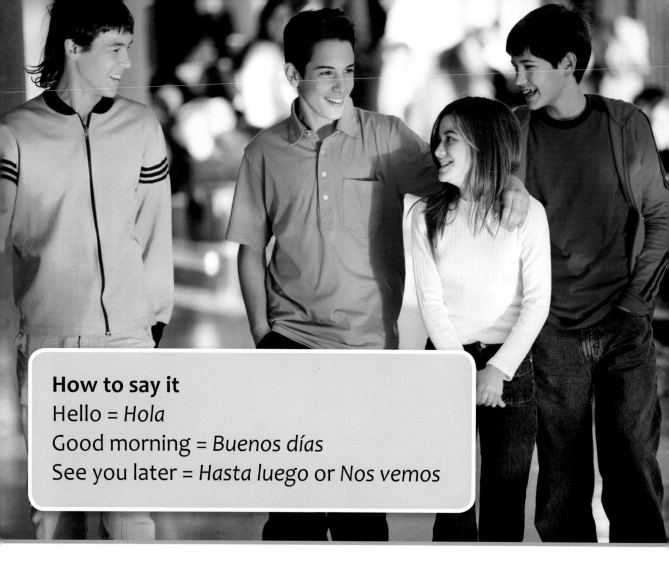

How to say it
Hello = *Hola*
Good morning = *Buenos días*
See you later = *Hasta luego* or *Nos vemos*

When people meet, they may say "*Hola*" or "*Buenos días*." "*Adiós*" means "Goodbye," but family and friends often say "*Hasta luego*" or "*Nos vemos*," too.

Talking About Yourself

When people meet others for the first time they usually give their name. They may say *"Me llamo Sarah"* or *"Mi nombre es Sarah."*

How to say it
I'm called… = *Me llamo …*
My name is = *Mi nombre es …*

How to say it
I'm from ... = *Soy de* ...
I live in ... = *Vivo en* ...

People often say where they are from, for example, "*Soy de España.*" ("I am from Spain.") They may say where they live, for example, "*Vivo en Valencia.*" ("I live in Valencia.")

Asking About Others

It is polite to ask other people about themselves. The first thing people usually ask is someone's name. They say "*¿Cómo te llamas?*"

How to say it
What's your name? = *¿Cómo te llamas?*

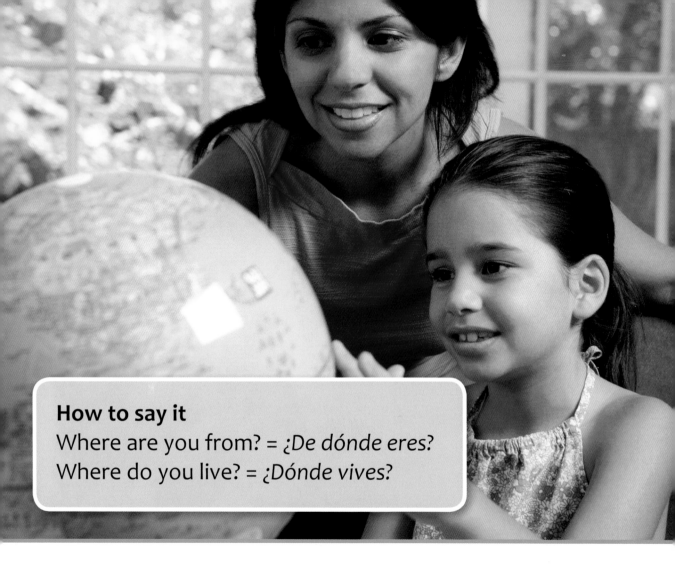

To ask someone where they are from
people usually say "*¿De dónde eres?*"
If they want to know where someone
lives they say "*¿Dónde vives?*"

At Home

A few people in Spain live in cave houses that are carved out of rock. Cave houses stay cool during the hot Spanish summers. They are very popular with tourists.

How to say it
house = *casa*
bedroom = *habitación*

living room = *sala*
kitchen = *cocina*
bathroom = *baño*

Some places in South America are very hot. Some people even sleep in hammocks instead of beds to stay cool. They are just as comfortable!

Family Life

South American families are often larger than families in the United States. There may be lots of brothers and sisters living with their mom and dad.

How to say it
mom = *mamá*
dad = *papá*
brother = *hermano*
sister = *hermana*

Grandparents often live with the whole family. Family celebrations, such as birthday parties, usually include aunts, uncles, and cousins, too.

At School

Many Spanish schools start at 9 o'clock and finish at 5 o'clock. Students have a long lunch break, when they can go home, eat, and have a short nap. This nap is called a *siesta*.

How to say it
school = *escuela*
student = *estudiante*
nap = *siesta*

How to say it
class = *clase*
morning = *mañana*
afternoon = *tarde*
vacations = *vacaciones*

In Bolivia, most children have classes
for four hours either in the morning
or in the afternoon, from Monday
to Saturday. Summer vacation is in
December and January.

Sports

Soccer is the main sport of Spain, and there are some great players. Spain won the Soccer World Cup in South Africa in 2010.

How to say it
sport = *deporte*
soccer = *fútbol*
ball = *pelota*
trophy = *trofeo*

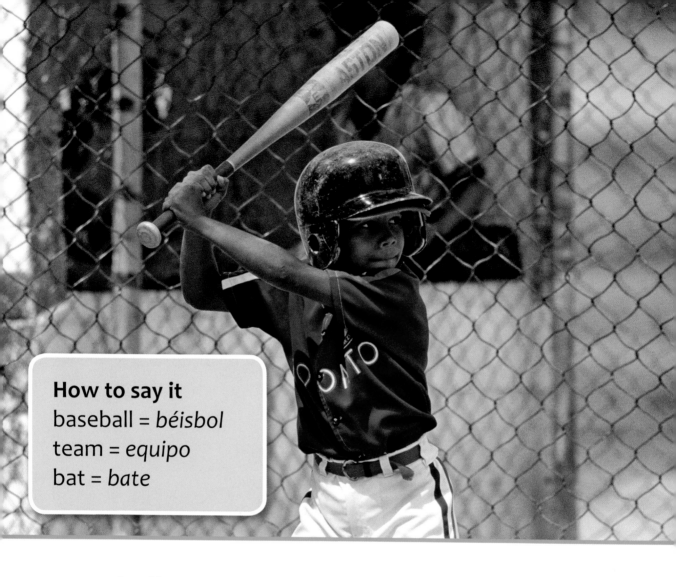

Baseball is popular in many South American countries, such as Venezuela. Some children play in baseball teams from a very young age.

Food

People in Spanish-speaking countries eat many different foods. In Spain, people love to eat small hot or cold snacks called *tapas* or *pinchos*.

How to say it
bread = *pan*
shrimp = *gambas*
ham = *jamón*
olives = *aceitunas*

In Mexico, food made with hot chillies is popular. A *tortilla* is a flat bread, often made from corn. *Tacos* are fried *tortillas* filled with spicy beans, meat, or cheese.

Clothes

Many people in Spanish-speaking countries relax in casual clothes like T-shirts and jeans. Some children wear school uniforms. For work, people wear dressier clothes like suits, shirts, and skirts.

How to say it
T-shirt = *camiseta*
jeans = *jeans or vaqueros*
uniform = *uniforme*

How to say it
suit = *traje*
hat = *bombín*
shawl = *chal*

In Bolivia, some women wear traditional
clothes in their day-to-day lives. They
often wear a bowler hat called a *bombín*.
They also wear a brightly colored shawl,
and a full skirt called a *pollera*.

Pronunciation Guide

English	Spanish	Pronunciation
afternoon	*tarde*	*tar-day*
aunt	*tía*	*tee-ah*
ball	*pelota*	*pay-lott-ah*
baseball	*béisbol*	*bay-is-boll*
bat	*bate*	*bah-tay*
bathroom	*baño*	*bah-nyo*
beans	*frijoles*	*free-hol-ays*
bed	*cama*	*cah-ma*
bedroom	*habitación*	*ah-bee-ta-thee-on*
bowler hat	*bombín*	*bom-bin*
bread	*pan*	*pan*
brother	*hermano*	*air-man-oh*
cheese	*queso*	*kay-so*
chilli	*chile*	*chee-lay*
class	*clase*	*clah-say*
cousin	*primo*	*pree-mo*
dad	*papá*	*pah-pah*
good morning	*buenos días*	*boo-ay-nos dee-as*
grandparent	*abuelo*	*ah-boo-ay-lo*
ham	*jamón*	*hah-mone*
hammock	*hamaca*	*ah-mah-cah*
hello	*hola*	*oh-lah*
house	*casa*	*cah-sah*
hug	*abrazo*	*ah-brah-tho*
I live in ...	*Vivo en ...*	*Bee-boh en*
I'm called ...	*Me llamo ...*	*May yah-mo*
I'm from ...	*Soy de ...*	*Soy day*

jeans	jeans	jeens
kiss	beso	bay-so
kitchen	cocina	coh-thee-nah
living room	sala	sah-lah
meat	carne	car-nay
mom	mamá	mah-mah
morning	mañana	mah-nyah-na
My name is …	Mi nombre es …	Mee nom-bray ess
nap	siesta	see-ess-tah
olives	aceitunas	ah-thay-too-nass
school	escuela	es-coo-ay-lah
see you later	hasta luego	as-tah loo-ay-go
see you later	nos vemos	nos bay-mos
shawl	chal	chal
shirt	camisa	cah-mee-sah
shrimp	gambas	gam-bass
sister	hermana	air-man-ah
soccer	fútbol	foot-boll
Spain	España	Es-pa-nya
sport	deporte	day-por-tay
student/pupil	estudiante	es-too-dee-an-tay
suit	traje	trah-hay
T-shirt	camiseta	cam-ee-say-tah
team	equipo	ay-kee-po
trophy	trofeo	tro-fay-o
uncle	tío	tee-o
uniform	uniforme	oo-nee-for-may
vacation	vacaciones	bah-cah-thee-on-ess
What's your name?	¿Cómo te llamas?	Co-moh tay yah-mas
Where are you from?	¿De dónde eres?	Day don-day air-ess
Where do you live?	¿Dónde vives?	Don-day bee-bess

Find Out More

Books

Brooks, Susie. *Let's Visit Spain*. New York: PowerKids Press, 2009.
Parker, Vic. *We're From Mexico*. Chicago:
      Heinemann Library, 2006.

Websites

kids.nationalgeographic.com/kids/places/find/spain/
www.bbc.co.uk/schools/primaryspanish/

Index

Meanings of the words on page 8

bicicleta = bicycle
tomate = tomato
fruta = fruit
familia = family
